CLASSROOM QUIZTIME

BOOK A

Peter Clutterbuck

USER FRIENDLY RESOURCES
EDUCATIONAL PUBLISHERS
www.userfr.com

Published by User Friendly Resources
Book No. 616A

TITLE
Book Name: Classroom Quiz Time
Book Number: 616A
ISBN: 978-1-86968-501-0
Published: 2008

AUTHOR
Peter Cluttterbuck

ACKNOWLEDGEMENTS
Designer: Codie Barnett
Illustrator: Codie Barnett
Editor: Ben Allan

PUBLISHER:
User Friendly Resources

United Kingdom Office	**New Zealand Office**	**Australian Office**
Freepost RRCB-ALHY-YAAA	PO Box 1820	PO Box 914
User Friendly Resources	Christchurch	Mascot, NSW 2020
Parkside Farm	Ph: 0508-500-393	Ph: 1800-553-890
Shortgate Lane	Fax: 0508-500-399	Fax: 1800-553-891
Lewes		
BN8 6DG		
Ph: 0845-450-7502		
Fax: 0845-688-0199		

WEBSITE: www.userfr.com
E-MAIL: info@userfr.com

User Friendly Resources specialises in publishing educational resources for teachers and students across a wide range of curriculum areas, at early childhood, primary and secondary levels. If you wish to know more about our resources, or if you think your resource ideas have publishing potential, please contact us at one of the above addresses.

CLASSROOM QUIZ TIME

ABOUT THIS BOOK...

Classroom Quiz Time contains a comprehensive array of quizzes designed to develop and extend students' general knowledge on a variety of topics and vital learning areas. The activity sheets may be used in numerous ways. These include

- for revision and testing of specific curriculum areas

- as extension activities for early finishers

- as a means of providing students with an opportunity to practise and enrich their research skills

- as challenging homework assignments or tasks

- as rainy day activities

- as a vehicle to create situations in which students must work together in small groups to solve and investigate information

- simply as fun activities

- as weekly research assignments

Students will find all the activities interesting and challenging. In many cases they may need to consult references such as a dictionary, thesaurus or encyclopedia. For this reason these activities are important to the development of independent study habits.

Oral quizzes are provided in Book A, along with a variety of response structures for the written quizzes. This is purposefully done to prevent students becoming bored with a stereotyped format.

Book A includes an oral quiz section as well as written answer questions for English and Maths.

CLASSROOM QUIZ TIME

TABLE OF CONTENTS

PART 1

ORAL QUIZZES

The following section contains general knowledge quizzes designed to be given orally to the class by the teacher or selected students.

The quizzes are also valuable for small group activities where a chosen student presents the questions to classmates.

Students write their responses on the "Answer Page" sheet. Answers are provided after each question so correction is made easy.

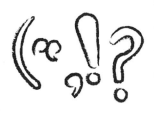

Teachers will find that the questions make general useful topic discussions and further research and this should be encouraged.

The quizzes could also be administered as a written activity if required. The answers included at the end of each line can be deleted using a white-out pencil.

The quiz questions have been carefully chosen and cover relevant curriculum areas. These areas include English, Mathematics, Social Studies, Health (our bodies), Science, Sport and General Knowledge.

There are 40 quizzes which roughly relates to one per week of the school year. Teachers therefore will find the quizzes valuable for revising and reinforcing their weekly classroom learning programmes, as challenges on rainy days, as a vehicle for stimulating brain-storming sessions or simply as enjoyable learning experiences.

ORAL QUIZZES

ORAL QUIZ 1

Date _____

1	What word beginning with d means the same as moist?	damp
2	What word beginning with l means the opposite of hate?	love
3	If we rearrange all the letters of lamp what tree can we get?	palm
4	What name do we give to the people who live in France?	French
5	Americans call it a faucet. What do we call it?	tap
6	What is the total when we add 2.5 and 2.5?	5
7	What number is 9 more than 188?	197
8	In what country is the city of Paris?	France
9	In what part of your body would you find an iris and retina?	eye
10	H_2O is the chemical name for what common substance?	water
11	What instrument is used to measure air pressure?	barometer
12	Who lost a glass slipper at the ball?	Cinderella
13	What kind of creature is a guppy?	fish
14	In what sport is the term LBW used?	cricket
15	In what sport do you use a racquet and shuttlecock?	badminton

ORAL QUIZ 2

Date _____

1	What word beginning with e means the same as mistake?	error
2	What word beginning with h means the opposite of miserable?	happy
3	If we rearrange all the letters of earth what organ can we make?	heart
4	What name do we give to people who live in Spain?	Spanish
5	We call it petrol. What do Americans call it?	gasoline
6	What is the largest three digit number you can write?	999
7	It is 9.45 am. What will be the time in twenty minutes?	10.05am
8	The Statue of Liberty can be found at the harbour of what city in the USA?	New York
9	What is the joint of your foot and leg called?	ankle
10	What name do we give to the line where earth and sky meet?	horizon
11	What word do we give to a reflected sound?	echo
12	Who cut off their tails with a carving knife?	the farmers' wife
13	What kind of creature is a sardine?	fish
14	In what sport are the terms love, deuce, and game used to score?	tennis
15	In what sport did Sir Donald Bradman excel?	cricket

6

ORAL QUIZZES

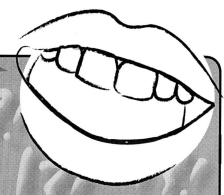

ORAL QUIZ 3

Date _____

1	What word beginning with s means the same as begin?	start
2	What word beginning with b means the opposite of sharp?	blunt
3	What kind of tree can you make by rearranging all the letters of cared?	cedar
4	What is the name we give to people who live in Wales?	Welsh
5	What name do we give to a food made from flour, salt and water?	damper
6	What is the sum when we add 45 and 55?	100
7	What is the difference between 80 and 35?	45
8	In what country is the Taj Mahal?	India
9	Lemons and oranges contain a lot of what vitamin?	vitamin C
10	What is the family name for mould, mushrooms and toadstools?	fungi
11	Is starboard to the left or right side of a ship?	right
12	What is the name given to a clock that tells the time of day by the sun?	sundial
13	What kind of living thing is a thoroughbred?	horse
14	Greg Norman, often called 'The Shark', is famous for which sport?	golf
15	What Olympic sport developed from throwing a spear?	javelin

ORAL QUIZ 4

Date _____

1	What is a word that means the same as conceal?	hide
2	What five letter word means the opposite of arrive?	leave
3	If you rearrange all the letters of flier what weapons can you get?	rifle
4	What name do we give to people who live in England?	English
5	What do people in the USA call a footpath?	sidewalk
6	What number is 5 less than 1002?	997
7	What is the largest 4 digit number you can write?	9999
8	The Eiffel Tower is in what great French city?	Paris
9	What gas is vital for life and for combustion?	oxygen
10	What do we call trees that retain their leaves all year?	evergreen
11	What is the star constellation on the Australian and New Zealand flags?	Southern Cross
12	What do we call an underwater projectile fired from a submarine?	torpedo
13	What kind of living thing is a goanna?	lizard
14	A very short foot race is known by what name?	sprint
15	The running race of the longest distance at the Olympics is called what?	marathon

ORAL QUIZZES

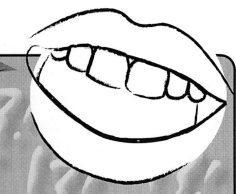

ORAL QUIZ 5

Date _____

1	What word beginning with s means the same as odour?	smell
2	What word beginning with p is the opposite of absent?	present
3	If you rearrange all the letters of shore what animal can you get?	horse
4	What name do we give to people who live in Holland?	Dutch
5	We call them lollies. What do people in the USA call them?	candy
6	What is 25 in Roman Numerals?	XXV
7	What number is 9 more than 9,998?	10,007
8	In what country is the ancient tomb called the Pyramid of Giza?	Egypt
9	What strong cords attach the ends of muscles to bones?	tendons
10	What is the name given to trees that lose their leaves?	deciduous
11	What is the term for removal of soil by wind and rain?	erosion
12	What is the name we give to a baby goose?	gosling
13	What kind of living thing is a cormorant?	bird
14	In what sport are the words freestyle and butterfly used?	swimming
15	Wood, putters and irons are used in what sport?	golf

ORAL QUIZ 6

Date _____

1	What three letter word beginning with o means the same as peculiar?	odd
2	What five letter word means the opposite of seldom?	often
3	If you rearrange all the letters of groan what instrument can you get?	organ
4	What word do we use for people who live in Denmark?	Danish
5	What is the American name for a tramp?	hobo
6	What two odd numbers between 5 and 12 add up to 18?	7, 11
7	How many sides has an octagon?	8
8	In what country is the mysterious group of rocks called Stonehenge found?	England
9	What is the name we use for the process of changing food in our bodies?	digestion
10	What is the name given to a unit of sound?	decibel
11	What is the name given to transference of heat waves?	radiation
12	Would you eat a beret or wear it?	wear it
13	What kind of living thing is a partridge?	bird
14	What sport requires you wear a parachute?	sky diving
15	What do we call a person who gives you out in cricket?	umpire

ORAL QUIZZES

ORAL QUIZ 7

Date _____

1	What five letter word beginning with b means the same as short?	brief
2	What is the opposite of interior?	exterior
3	If you rearrange all the letters of fringe what body part can you make?	finger
4	What name do we give to people who live in Iraq?	Iraqi
5	What do Americans call university?	college
6	What are the total number of days in Spring?	91
7	It is 7.20 pm. What will the time be in 1 ½ hours?	8.50 pm
8	The Red Square is in what Russian city?	Moscow
9	What are molars and incisors?	teeth
10	A material which can conduct heat or electricity is called what?	conductor
11	On what would you find petals, sepals and stamens?	flowers
12	What is the first month of Autumn in the Southern Hemisphere?	March
13	What kind of living thing is an orange roughy?	fish
14	Scrum, ruck and drop goal are terms used in which sport?	rugby
15	Only one player per team can touch the ball with their hands in which sport?	soccer

ORAL QUIZ 8

Date _____

1	What four letter word means the same as cease?	stop
2	The opposite of contract is what?	expand
3	If you rearrange all the letters of stinted what occupation can you get?	dentist
4	What name do we give to people who live in Switzerland?	Swiss
5	What is the American word for timetable?	schedule
6	Which is larger, 3/4 or 9/12?	they are the same
7	What is the difference between 5 and 1.5?	3.5
8	With what country do we associate the shamrock and harp?	Ireland
9	The hard white covering of our teeth is called by what name?	enamel
10	What do we call a creature that lives in both water and land?	amphibian
11	What is the name given to materials that will not conduct electricity or heat?	insulator
12	What is a sundae?	ice-cream
13	What kind of living thing is a sycamore?	tree
14	A bat we use for playing tennis is known by what name?	racquet
15	What do you pass to the next runner in a relay race?	baton

9

ORAL QUIZZES

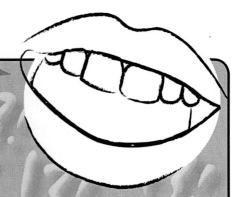

ORAL QUIZ 9

Date _____

1	What three letter word means the same as to excavate?	dig
2	What six letter word beginning with r means the opposite of punishment?	reward
3	If you rearrange all the letters of ample what tree can you make?	maple
4	What name do we give to people who live in Cyprus?	Cypriots
5	We call them biscuits. What do people in the USA call them?	cookies
6	What is 4^2 minus 2^2?	12
7	What is the value of 3 in the number written as 2-5-6-3-4-4?	300
8	What is the world's largest island?	Greenland
9	How many teeth does an adult human have in a full set?	32
10	What imaginary line of latitude passes through northern Australia, southern Africa and South America?	Tropic of Capricorn
11	What do we call an animal's winter sleep?	hibernation
12	What word taken from the name of an animal means embarrassed or bashful?	sheepish
13	What kind of living thing is a dromedary?	camel
14	What is the edge of a cricket oval called?	boundary
15	In what sport is the word knockout used?	boxing

ORAL QUIZ 10

Date _____

1	What word beginning with a means the same as height?	altitude
2	What word beginning with m means the opposite of ancient?	modern
3	If you rearrange all the letters of solemn what fruit can you make?	lemons
4	What name do we give to people who live in Pakistan?	Pakistanis
5	What do Americans call a tram?	streetcar
6	What is the value of 7 in the number written as 2-1-7-4-8-6?	7000
7	Round 153 to the nearest hundred.	200
8	In what country is a lake called Loch Ness?	Scotland (United Kingdom)
9	What is the gas that forms the major part of the air we breathe?	nitrogen
10	What is the planet nearest the Sun?	Mercury
11	What season comes in September, October and November in the Southern Hemisphere?	Spring
12	To what family of animals does a puma belong?	felines (cats)
13	What kind of living thing is a locust?	insect
14	What sport needs a springing board?	diving
15	In what Olympic sport do you throw a simple iron ball?	shot put

10

ORAL QUIZZES

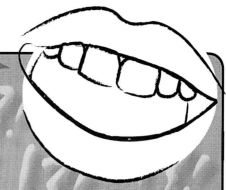

ORAL QUIZ 11

Date _____

1	What word beginning with c means the middle?	centre
2	A four letter word meaning the opposite of entrance is what?	exit
3	If you rearrange all the letters of could what word can you make?	cloud
4	What name do we give to people who live in Ireland?	Irish
5	What is the Aboriginal name for Ayres Rock?	Uluru
6	Round 2,468 to the nearest thousand.	2000
7	What are all the factors of 12?	1, 12, 2, 6, 3, 4
8	In what Asian country is Mount Everest?	Nepal
9	In what part of the body is the Adam's Apple?	throat
10	What do we call a body that circles our Earth?	satellite
11	What instrument is used to show us directions?	compass
12	A cygnet is the baby of what bird?	swan
13	What kind of living thing is a dalmatian?	dog
14	What is a boat with sails often used for racing called?	yacht
15	What is the Maori name for Mount Cook?	Aoraki

ORAL QUIZ 12

Date _____

1	What four letter word beginning with c means frigid?	cold
2	What word beginning with f is the opposite of smile?	frown
3	If you rearrange all the letters of drive what occupation can you make?	diver
4	What name do we give to people who live in Tibet?	Tibetans
5	What is a joey?	baby kangaroo
6	Write the word for this ordinal number: 15th.	fifteenth
7	What in Roman numerals was the symbol for 50?	L
8	In what country is the Grand Canyon of Colorado?	USA
9	The bean shaped organs that flush away waste products are called what?	kidneys
10	What is the silicon chip a component of?	computer
11	What instrument measures heat and cold?	thermometer
12	Would you eat a lozenge or wear it?	eat it
13	What kind of living thing is a chameleon?	lizard
14	You need a table, bat, net and ball to play what sport?	table tennis
15	A slalom is a move used in what sport?	skiing

11

ORAL QUIZZES

ORAL QUIZ 13

Date _____

1	What word beginning with a means something happening yearly?	annual
2	What four letter word beginning with d means the opposite to admit?	deny
3	If you rearrange all the letters of listen what decoration can you make?	tinsel
4	What name do we give to people who live in Europe?	Europeans
5	What kind of creature is a galah?	bird
6	How many years in 3.5 decades?	35
7	The three books I borrowed each had 160 pages. How many pages altogether is this?	480
8	With what country do we associate emus and kangaroos?	Australia
9	Plasma and corpuscles are part of what substance in our bodies?	blood
10	What do we call a device that magnifies tiny objects?	microscope
11	What is used to measure wind speed?	anemometer
12	From what fruit do we get cider?	apples
13	What kind of living thing is a sturgeon?	fish
14	The organisation FIFA runs what sport?	soccer
15	What sport needs bats, balls and bases?	baseball

ORAL QUIZ 14

Date _____

1	What word ending in ful means the same as cautious?	careful
2	What five letter word is the opposite of hollow?	solid
3	If you rearrange all the letters of bleat what furniture can you make?	table
4	What name do we give to people who live in Israel?	Israelis
5	The explorer Abel Tasman was from what country?	The Netherlands (Holland)
6	An athlete completed only 860 metres of a 2000 metre race. How far did he have to go to the finish?	1140m
7	Mike spent $3.90 of his $10.00. How much has he left?	$6.10
8	With what country do we associate mounted police and a maple leaf?	Canada
9	A thick walled blood vessel is known by what name?	artery
10	What instrument measures angles in surveying?	theodolite
11	What do we call lines that join places of equal pressure on a weather map?	isobar
12	In what country is the kilt a traditional item of clothing?	Scotland (United Kingdom)
13	What kind of living thing is a termite?	insect
14	The leader of a sporting team is known by what name?	captain
15	The America's Cup is a famous race for what water craft?	yachts

ORAL QUIZZES

ORAL QUIZ 15

Date _____

1	What word beginning with p means courteous?	polite
2	What word beginning with d means the opposite of giant?	dwarf
3	If you rearrange all the letters of hectare what occupation can you make?	teacher
4	What name do we give to people from Norway?	Norwegian
5	Beginning with q, what do we call a creature with four legs?	quadruped
6	Mike lives 4 km from school. How far does he travel to and from school in 4 weeks?	160 km
7	How many 6s in 96?	16
8	In what country would we see the Acropolis?	Greece
9	What is the name given to the transferring of blood from one person to another?	transfusion
10	What instrument is used to measure the force of an earthquake?	seismograph
11	What is the molten rock flowing from a volcano called?	lava
12	How many singers make up a duet?	two
13	Would you eat tofu or wear it?	eat it
14	A hundred runs in cricket is called a what?	century
15	Which is larger: an Indian or African elephant?	African

ORAL QUIZ 16

Date _____

1	What word beginning with d means sleepy?	drowsy
2	What ten letter word means the opposite of genuine?	artificial
3	If you rearrange all the letters of stripe what occupation can you make?	priest
4	What name do we give to people who live in the Italian province of Venice?	Venetians
5	What do we call a stand that has three legs?	tripod
6	2 ¾ plus 1 ¼ equals how many quarters?	16/4
7	Write 60/100 as a decimal fraction.	0.6
8	In what Italian city is the Leaning Tower?	Pisa
9	Ventricles and auricles are part of what important body organ?	heart
10	What word do we use to describe a plant or animal that has completely disappeared from earth?	extinct
11	What do we call the skeletons of plants and animals found in rocks?	fossils
12	For what is Igor Sikorsky remembered?	helicopter pioneer
13	Caviar is the eggs of what kind of creature?	fish
14	In what sport must you be careful not to serve foot faults?	tennis
15	A hole in one is a great shot in what sport?	golf

13

ORAL QUIZZES

ORAL QUIZ 17

Date _____

1	What eight letter word beginning with e means huge?	enormous
2	What word beginning with m is the opposite of divide?	multiply
3	For what whole word is fridge a shortening of?	refrigerator
4	Beginning with u, what is a one wheeled cycle?	unicycle
5	If you rearrange all the letters of words what weapon can you make?	sword
6	Write fourteen tenths as a fraction.	14/10 or 1 4/10 or 1.4
7	Write seven tenths as a decimal fraction.	0.7
8	What country forms a border with the USA to the north?	Canada
9	The major organs in humans used to breathe are called what?	lungs
10	The three basic kinds of rock are igneous, metaphoric, and what?	sedimentary
11	What is the name given to an animal that eats only meat?	carnivore
12	What do we call the air surrounding the earth?	atmosphere
13	What kind of living thing is a kauri?	tree
14	The pits are resting places for what sport?	car racing
15	The Commonwealth is an organisation of former colonies of what country?	England

ORAL QUIZ 18

Date _____

1	What four letter word means the same as generous?	kind
2	What five letter word means the opposite of expensive?	cheap
3	If you rearrange all the letters of rialto what occupation can you make?	tailor
4	For what word is gym a shortening of?	gymnasium
5	Beginning with b, what is a flat bottomed boat for transporting goods?	barge
6	Double 57 ¼.	114 ½
7	What number is 500 less than 10,000?	9500
8	The kiwi and fern are associated with what country?	New Zealand
9	By what do we call the movement of blood around our bodies?	circulation
10	What is the name we give to reflections of objects seen in a mirror?	image
11	The three primary colours in paint are red, blue and what other?	yellow
12	What kind of creature is a hornet?	wasp
13	What kind of living thing is an acacia?	tree
14	What is a sport that needs a hoop and net?	netball or basketball
15	What sport needs good waves for riding?	surfing

14

ORAL QUIZZES

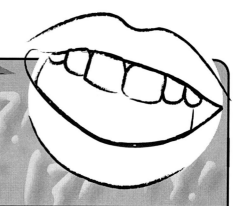

ORAL QUIZ 19

Date _____

1	What six letter word beginning with r means strong?	robust
2	What six letter word is the opposite of wide?	narrow
3	If you rearrange all the letters of prides what creature can you make?	spider
4	For what is the word ammo a shortening of?	ammunition
5	What word beginning with c means the goods carried on a ship?	cargo
6	Halve 126 ½.	63 ¼
7	What is the sum of 26 plus 12?	38
8	In what country is Mt Fuji?	Japan
9	A doctor uses what instrument to listen to your heart beat?	stethoscope
10	What do we call a mirror that bulges outwards?	convex
11	What is a lodestone?	magnet
12	How many stars on the USA flag?	fifty
13	Would you strum a gondola or row it?	row it
14	What is the small round section in the middle of a dartboard called?	bullseye
15	In what sport do you need bows and arrows?	archery

ORAL QUIZ 20

Date _____

1	What four letter word means the same as detest?	hate
2	What five letter word is the opposite of true?	false
3	If you rearrange all the letters of clasp what body part can you make?	scalp
4	For what is the word photo a shortening?	photograph
5	Beginning with h, what is a vehicle for transporting deceased people?	hearse
6	What is the product of 300 and 10?	3000
7	¼ of 80 equals one hundred minus what number?	80
8	In what country is the Great Wall?	China
9	What are the smallest of all blood vessels called?	capillaries
10	What do we call a band of all the colours in light?	spectrum
11	What is the name we give to a very powerful, focussed light beam?	laser
12	How many eggs in a baker's dozen?	thirteen
13	What kind of living thing is a grevillea?	plant
14	How many pins do you knock over in bowling?	ten
15	The Olympic Games are held every how many years?	four

ORAL QUIZZES

ORAL QUIZ 21

Date _____

1	What word beginning with e means to anticipate?	expect
2	What word beginning with w is the opposite of poverty?	wealth
3	If you rearrange all the letters of street what dog can you make?	setter
4	For what word is burger a shortening of?	hamburger
5	What is another name for a car for hire?	taxi
6	I had $20 and spent $6.85. How much have I left?	$13.15
7	Four students each have $8.65. How much do they have altogether?	$34.60
8	What is the northernmost state of the USA?	Alaska
9	What is the name given to the waste liquid removed from our bodies?	urine
10	If you mix blue and yellow paint what colour will you get?	green
11	What is the name we give a piece of glass that breaks white light into its colours?	prism
12	What kind of creature is an ocelot?	(wild) cat
13	What kind of living thing is a tarantula?	spider
14	What do we call a person who rides a horse in races?	jockey
15	What do we call a bouncing platform used in sports?	trampoline

ORAL QUIZ 22

Date _____

1	What six letter word beginning with f means the same as ferocious?	fierce
2	What six letter word beginning with o is the opposite of transparent?	opaque
3	If you rearrange all the letters of softer what word can you make?	forest
4	The huge fleet known as the Spanish Armada attempted to invade which country?	England
5	What name do we give to a person travelling on foot?	pedestrian
6	Is 7 a factor of 392? (Yes or No)	Yes
7	What are the factors of 40?	1, 40, 2, 20, 4, 10, 5, 8
8	In what English city is the clock tower Big Ben?	London
9	Groups of cells that make secretions called hormones are what?	glands
10	What do we call the glowing piece of metal in a light globe?	filament
11	What name is given to materials that allow light to pass through?	transparent
12	On what date is New Year's Day each year?	January 1
13	In what century was the telephone invented?	19th
14	What is the capital of Fiji?	Suva
15	In what sport do we throw rope circles over a peg?	quoits

ORAL QUIZZES

ORAL QUIZ 23

Date _____

1	What 4 letter word beginning with g means a donation or present?	gift
2	What word beginning with p is the opposite of temporary?	permanent
3	If you rearrange all the letters of enlarge what army rank can you get?	general
4	For what word is vet a shortening of?	veterinary surgeon
5	Beginning with b, what is a two piece swim suit?	bikini
6	What name do we give to an angle less than ninety degrees?	acute
7	When two halves of something are exactly the same what do we call this?	symmetry
8	In what country is the volcano Mt Vesuvius located?	Italy
9	The liquid secreted by glands in the mouth is known by what name?	saliva
10	What is the name we use for reusing waste materials?	recycling
11	What is the name given to an animal that hunts another?	predator
12	What name do we give to a female fox?	vixen
13	Is an elver a baby rabbit or baby eel?	eel
14	What sport first played by native Americans uses a net?	lacrosse
15	For what sport were John McEnroe and Martina Navratilova famous?	tennis

ORAL QUIZ 24

Date _____

1	What word beginning with v means the same as conceited?	vain
2	What word beginning with g is the opposite of sudden?	gradual
3	If you rearrange all the letters of filter what dessert can you make?	trifle
4	For what word is rhino a shortening?	rhinoceros
5	On what part of your body would you wear a mitten?	hand
6	What name do we give to an angle of ninety degrees?	right angle
7	What is the boiling point of water on a Celsius scale?	100°C
8	What is the capital city of Spain?	Madrid
9	A cochlea, drum and lobe are parts of what body organ?	ear
10	What word beginning with t is used to describe poisonous chemicals?	toxins
11	What beginning with c is the general weather in an area?	climate
12	What do we call a frightening dream?	nightmare
13	Is a leveret a baby hare or bear?	hare
14	From what wood are cricket bats mainly made?	willow
15	In what Olympic sport do you throw a flat disc?	discus

17

ORAL QUIZZES

ORAL QUIZ 25

Date _____

1	What word beginning with z means the same as nought?	zero
2	What word beginning with m is the opposite of conceited?	modest
3	Rearrange all the letters of charm to get what soldiers do.	march
4	What is the shortened form we write for perambulator?	pram
5	What tough cloth is used to make jeans?	denim
6	It is 5.15pm. What will the time be in 4 hours and 10 minutes?	9.25pm
7	Today is the twenty-eighth of April. What will the date be in 5 days time?	May 3
8	What Italian city is famous for its canals and gondolas?	Venice
9	Our four tastes are bitter, sour, salt and what other one?	sweet
10	What do we call long periods of no rainfall?	droughts
11	What beginning with i is a large device for burning waste?	incinerator
12	What bird is known for its homing instincts?	pigeons
13	Would you drink linament or rub it on your body?	rub it on
14	In what sport do people compete at Wimbledon in the UK?	tennis
15	The Ashes are played for in what sport?	cricket

ORAL QUIZ 26

Date _____

1	What word beginning with c means a metropolis?	city
2	What word beginning with i is the opposite of superior?	inferior
3	What word meaning 'not dirty' can you make from the letters of lance?	clean
4	What is the shortening we write for omnibus?	bus
5	What name do we give to a container for coins?	purse
6	What is 5.30 in 24 hour time?	1730 hours
7	How many kilograms in 5 and a quarter metric tonnes?	5250
8	What American city is famous for movie making?	Hollywood (Los Angeles)
9	How many bones do our bodies have?	206
10	The word given to "faster than the speed of sound" is what?	supersonic
11	The force that holds everything on the Earth's surface is called what?	gravity
12	What is the meat of a deer called?	venison
13	An acorn is the seed of what kind of tree?	oak
14	What sport is played by scoring points again four walls?	squash
15	Phar Lap was famous for what sport?	horse racing

18

ORAL QUIZZES

ORAL QUIZ 27

Date _____

1	If you have a query you would ask a what?	question
2	What 6 letter word is the opposite of awake?	asleep
3	What rock can you make from all the letters of tales?	slate
4	What is the shortened form we write for influenza?	flu
5	We call them pigs. What do farmers in the USA call them?	hogs
6	What is the volume of a shape 3cm long, 3cm wide and 3cm high?	27 cm^3
7	What is the area of a square with sides of 9 centimetres?	81cm^2
8	What is the capital city of Canada?	Ottawa
9	By what name are the bones that make up our spines called?	vertebrae
10	The path of a planet around the Sun is called its what?	orbit
11	What do we call a machine for producing electricity?	generator
12	What is the meat of a sheep called?	mutton or lamb
13	The only two mammals to lay eggs are the echidna and the what?	platypus
14	In what sport do you strike an object called a puck?	ice hockey
15	In what sport do you use reels, hooks and sinkers?	angling/fishing

ORAL QUIZ 28

Date _____

1	What word beginning with l means to free something?	liberate
2	What 5 letter word is the opposite of heavy?	light
3	What direction can you make by using all the letters of thorn?	north
4	What is the shortened form we use for zoological gardens?	zoo
5	What name do we give to a leather container for notes of money?	wallet
6	What is the perimeter of a rectangle with sides of 14cm and 8cm?	44cm
7	What is our number for the Roman number LXV?	65
8	What is Egypt's capital city?	Cairo
9	Saliva helps turn food starch into what easily digested food?	sugar
10	What is the name we give to the flow of electricity along a wire?	circuit
11	What do we call a mixture of two or more metals?	alloy
12	Who presides over a court of law and gives judgements?	judge magistrate
13	How many legs has a weevil?	six
14	What endangered New Zealand bird is the world's only flightless parrot?	kakapo
15	In what Olympic sport do you throw a metal ball on a chain?	hammer throw

ORAL QUIZZES

ORAL QUIZ 29

Date _____

1	If something is azure what colour is it?	blue
2	What 4 letter word beginning with d means the opposite of dusk?	dawn
3	What food can we make from all the letters of west?	stew
4	What is the shortened form we write for All Hallow's Evening?	Halloween
5	Beginning with c what is the name for knives, forks, spoons etc?	cutlery
6	How many minutes in 6 ½ hours?	390
7	How many days in 8 fortnights?	112
8	What Pacific island is a state of America?	Hawaii
9	How many senses does the human body have?	five
10	What is the name we give to electricity generated by the sun?	solar power
11	What do we call the gaseous form of water?	vapour
12	What do we call the first showing of a movie or play?	premiere
13	What kind of creature is a thrip?	insect
14	In what sport do you use horses, mallet and a ball?	polo
15	What is the two word name we give to Formula One races?	Grand Prix

ORAL QUIZ 30

Date _____

1	A word beginning with c which means serene is what?	calm
2	What six letter word beginning with u is the opposite of common?	unique
3	What animal can we make from all the letters of toast?	stoat
4	What is the shortened form we use for God Be With You?	goodbye
5	Beginning with h, what is a large basket with a lid for a picnic?	hamper
6	What is the cost of 12kg at $1.40 a kilogram?	$16.80
7	What number is 40 more than 9990?	10,030
8	What is the capital city of Greece?	Athens
9	What is the breaking of a bone called?	fracture
10	What is the only natural satellite of our Earth?	the Moon
11	What is the name given to gigantic groups of stars?	galaxies
12	What do we call a daytime performance of a play or movie?	matinee
13	What kind of creature is a puffin?	bird
14	In what country were the first Olympic Games held?	Greece
15	In what sport do we use the terms pairs, fours and eights?	rowing

20

ORAL QUIZZES

ORAL QUIZ 31

Date _____

1	What word beginning with u means to comprehend something?	understand
2	What word beginning with a is the opposite of repel?	attract
3	What body part can we make from all the letters of swine?	sinew
4	What is claustrophobia a fear of?	enclosed spaces
5	Beginning with g, what do we call an extremely clever person?	genius
6	What is 10,004 minus 8?	9996
7	What is double 84.7?	169.4
8	In what continent are Vietnam and Thailand?	Asia
9	The smallest bone in the body is found in what organ?	ear
10	What is the name given to the total amount of matter in an object?	mass
11	What word beginning with i means the tendency of a body to stay at rest or stay moving?	inertia
12	Beginning with h, what is another name for a mouth organ?	harmonica
13	Is an oriole a kind of dog or bird?	bird
14	In what sport is a ball hit through hoops with a mallet?	croquet
15	The words kitty, mat and ends are associated with what sport?	lawn bowls

ORAL QUIZ 32

Date _____

1	What word beginning with d means the same as squalid?	dirty
2	Would clumsy or smooth be the opposite of graceful?	clumsy
3	What word can be made from rearranging all the letters of rustle?	result
4	For what is arachnophobia a fear of?	spiders
5	Beginning with f, what do we call pieces of fish with the bones removed?	fillet
6	What is 5 minus 1 and 2/3?	3 1/3
7	What is the sum of $4.70 and $8.35?	$13.05
8	In what continent are the countries of Egypt and Libya?	Africa
9	The harmful sticky substance that affects teeth is called what?	plaque
10	What word is used to describe increased speed of an object?	acceleration
11	What do we call animals that feed their young on milk?	mammals
12	Beginning with l, what is a soothing song to get babies to sleep?	lullaby
13	Is a budgerigar a kind of eagle or kind of parrot?	parrot
14	The three medals presented at the Olympics are gold, silver and what?	bronze
15	In what sport is a long pole and high bar used?	pole vaulting

ORAL QUIZZES

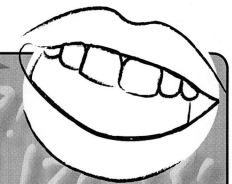

ORAL QUIZ 33

Date _____

1	What word beginning with t means to taunt someone?	tease
2	The opposite to success is what word?	failure
3	If we rearranged all the letters of cores what word can we make?	score
4	What is aquaphobia a fear of?	water
5	What makes redivider and racecar special words?	they are palindromes (same forwards and backwards)
6	What is the value of 5 in the number written as 4-5-6-8-1-0-0?	500,000
7	Write 0.2 as a common fraction.	2/10 or 1/5
8	What is the world's smallest continent?	Australia
9	What is the name given for the liquid in which blood floats?	serum
10	What is the word we use for the force that creates heat when two bodies rub together?	friction
11	To what rod are the wheels on a cart attracted?	axle
12	What do we call a group of four musicians?	quartet
13	Would you eat a lychee or wear it?	eat it
14	In what sport is there a player called a wicketkeeper?	cricket
15	A velodrome is used for what sport?	cycling

ORAL QUIZ 34

Date _____

1	What three letter word beginning with f means an enemy?	foe
2	Give a word that is the opposite of cautious that also begins with c?	careless
3	What rock can we make from all the letters of ramble?	marble
4	For what is zoophobia a fear of?	animals
5	What makes the word hijinks special?	three dotted letters in a row
6	Is 3/8 a proper or improper fraction?	proper
7	Sally's foal has lived for 567 days. How many weeks is that?	81
8	What large island lies south-east of India?	Sri Lanka
9	The chemical melanin determines the colour of what part of the human body?	skin
10	What, beginning with v, cause sound?	vibrations
11	Will magnets with opposite poles nearby attract or repel each other?	attract
12	How many years in a decade?	ten
13	Is a sidewinder a reptile or fish?	reptile
14	A farrier is often needed in what sport?	horse racing
15	In what sport is the term deuce used?	tennis

ORAL QUIZZES

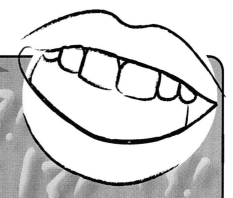

ORAL QUIZ 35

Date _____

1	What word beginning with j means youthful?	juvenile
2	A word that has 6 letters and begins with l and is the opposite of solid is what?	liquid
3	What precious stones can we make from all the letters of bruise?	rubies
4	What is a word that would best complete this: Flour is to mill as beer is to	brewery
5	What do Americans call a lift in a tall building?	elevator
6	What is the remainder when you divide 186 by 9?	6
7	The city of Perth was founded in 1829. How old will it be in 2014?	185 years
8	In what continent are the countries of Bolivia and Brazil?	South America
9	The cortex and cerebellum are part of what body organ?	brain
10	What are the three states of matter?	solids, liquids, gases
11	What do we call it when water is so heated it violently bubbles?	boiling
12	What do we call a room for passengers on a cruise liner?	cabin
13	What kind of creature is a beagle?	dog
14	A well known sport played on ice is what?	ice hockey
15	A sportsperson who is not paid for playing is called what?	amateur

ORAL QUIZ 36

Date _____

1	What word beginning with s means acute?	sharp
2	What word also beginning with m is the opposite of maximum?	minimum
3	What word can we get by rearranging all the letters of seaside?	disease
4	What word would best complete this sentence – fish is to water as bird is to	air
5	Beginning with c, what name do we give to an Aboriginal ceremony?	corroboree
6	What is the Roman numeral for 28?	XXVIII
7	What prime number between 10 and 20 has digits that add to 10?	19
8	In what continent are the countries of Germany and Italy?	Europe
9	What is the organ that pumps blood around the body?	heart
10	Protons, neutrons and electrons make up what tiny particles of matter?	atoms
11	What is the name we give to the process of objects increasing in size when heated?	expansion
12	How many wings has a biplane?	two
13	Is a jaguar herbivorous or carnivorous?	carnivorous
14	Lords in the UK is a famous ground for what sport?	cricket
15	How many players are there in a netball team?	seven

ORAL QUIZZES

ORAL QUIZ 37

Date _____

1	What word beginning with g means the same as a device?	gadget
2	What word beginning with d is the opposite of marriage?	divorce
3	What word can we make from all the letters of rinse?	reins
4	What two words make up the contraction you've?	you have
5	Beginning with d, what is an Aboriginal musical instrument?	didgeridoo
6	Round 17,294 to the nearest 1000.	17000
7	What is 8^2 plus 4^2?	80
8	In what ocean are the islands of Fiji and Tonga?	Pacific
9	Hereditary traits are controlled by what things that are passed on?	genes
10	What do we call two or more atoms joined together?	molecules
11	What do we call a change that is irreversible i.e. paper burning?	chemical change
12	Who lost their sheep and didn't know where to find them?	Little Bo Peep
13	Are Siamese and Burmese kinds of cats or dogs?	cats
14	If you score a duck in cricket how many runs have you made?	none
15	What is the world's second-highest mountain?	K2

ORAL QUIZ 38

Date _____

1	What word beginning with p means the same as rind?	peel
2	What word beginning with s is the opposite of intoxicated?	sober
3	What writing implement can we make from all the letters of staple?	pastel
4	What two words make up the contraction we'd?	we would or we had
5	What name is given to places far from the city in Australia?	outback
6	How many eggs in 9 and a 1/4 dozen?	111
7	Write eight million, six hundred and eighty nine thousand and seven in figures.	8,689,007
8	What is the longest river in Africa?	Nile
9	A fatty substance credited with blocking human arteries is called what?	cholesterol
10	What is the name we give to fuels such as coal, oil and natural gas?	fossil fuels
11	What name do we give to foods made up of carbon, hydrogen and oxygen?	carbohydrates
12	A pawn, rook and king are associated with what board game?	chess
13	Which of these has scales, a viper or a toucan?	viper
14	The sports teams known as the Kiwis and the Kangaroos play what sport?	rugby league
15	What is the name given to an ice covered space for skating?	rink

ORAL QUIZZES

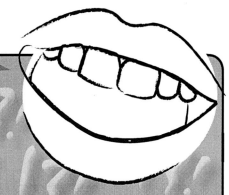

ORAL QUIZ 39

Date _____

1	What word beginning with sh means the same as astute or clever?	shrewd
2	What word ending in ful is the opposite of senseless?	meaningful
3	What word can we make by rearranging all the letters of lament?	mantle or mental
4	What two words make up the contraction we're?	we are
5	Beginning with h, what is a song of praise to God?	hymn
6	What is the product of 5 and 80.5?	402.5
7	What is one million minus one hundred and fifty thousand?	850,000
8	In what continent did the Aztecs and Incas once live?	South America
9	Our skin contains glands that help excrete waste and water. These are called what?	sweat glands
10	What is the name we give to the dumping of chemical and other wastes?	pollution
11	What do we call rocks changed in nature by forces like heat, pressure and tectonics?	metamorphic
12	In what game can Mayfair and Park Lane be found?	Monopoly
13	To what family of living things does a cicada belong?	insects
14	In what sport do the Wallabies excel?	rugby
15	What is the roped area for boxing called?	ring

ORAL QUIZ 40

Date _____

1	What word beginning with j means to deride?	jeer
2	What word beginning with r means the opposite of amplify?	reduce
3	Can you use all the letters of conversationalist to make a person who likes to conserve things?	conservationalist
4	What two words make up the contraction aren't?	are not
5	Beginning with ch, what name do we give to a group of singers?	choir
6	How many days in February 2016?	29 days
7	What is the total when you add all the odd numbers between 10 and 20?	75
8	What country has a border with the USA to its north?	Mexico
9	What is the name given to the breathing organs of fish?	gills
10	What are the weights of precious minerals measured in?	carats
11	What word is used to describe a volcano that has not erupted for some years but may do again?	dormant
12	What do we call an optical illusion often seen in the desert?	mirage
13	What kind of living things are mackerels, piranhas and carp?	fish
14	What sport consists of cycling, swimming and running?	triathlon
15	How many events do athletes compete in during a decathlon?	ten

25

ORAL QUIZZES

ORAL QUIZZES ANSWER SHEET

QUIZ NUMBER	Date _____
1	
2	
3	
4	
5	
6	
7	
8	
9	
10	
11	
12	
13	
14	
15	
Total correct	

QUIZ NUMBER	Date _____
1	
2	
3	
4	
5	
6	
7	
8	
9	
10	
11	
12	
13	
14	
15	
Total correct	

QUIZ NUMBER	Date _____
1	
2	
3	
4	
5	
6	
7	
8	
9	
10	
11	
12	
13	
14	
15	
Total correct	

QUIZ NUMBER	Date _____
1	
2	
3	
4	
5	
6	
7	
8	
9	
10	
11	
12	
13	
14	
15	
Total correct	

PART 2

WRITTEN QUIZZES

ENGLISH AND MATHS

The following quizzes can be photocopied and distributed to the students.

They represent core learning areas of the classroom programme.

They an be used to develop

1   interest in a subject area

2   as a challenging research project

3   as rainy day activities

4   as small group assignments

5   as revision and consolidation for specific areas within core subjects content

6   as interesting home/school projects

The answers should be written on the sheets. Answer pages for self/class correction are provided on the back of this section.

To add interest and challenge, small groups may work together to complete particular quizzes.

27

WRITTEN QUIZZES

DATE _____
NAME _____
_____

WORD MEANINGS 1

ENGLISH

Choose a word from the box that can replace the bold words.
Write it in the space on the right.

1	The **body of the ship** was made of steel.	
2	The **wood for building** has been delivered.	
3	As she hadn't eaten all day Sally was **very hungry.**	
4	The water came in a **sudden rush.**	
5	We prayed in the **small church.**	
6	The man **washed and ironed** the clothes.	
7	We left the plates on the **narrow shelf.**	
8	He was so scared he began to **shake with fear.**	
9	The birds picked up and ate all the **bits of bread.**	
10	These utensils are **helpful to have.**	
11	The light began to **become less bright.**	
12	I ate the **skin of the apple.**	
13	It is rude to **look hard** at other people.	
14	She accidentally burnt the **roof of her mouth.**	
15	These goods are **of little cost.**	
16	The **precious stone** was stolen by the thieves.	
17	She felt **very sleepy.**	
18	The new ship had been **set afloat.**	
19	The heavy weight landed with a **dull sound.**	
20	They **made a hole in** the butter with a knife.	

famished	stare	hull	laundered	fade
chapel	jewel	gush	useful	pierced
ledge	drowsy	peel	timber	launched
palate	thud	crumbs	cheap	tremble

TOTAL

/20

28

WRITTEN QUIZZES

DATE _____

NAME _____

WORD MEANINGS 2

ENGLISH

Choose a word on the right that has the same meaning as the bold words.

1	The ring has a precious **red stone.**		still
2	The **sweet smelling vine** grew in the yard.		shod
3	The horse was **fitted with shoes.**		margin
4	The **regular beat** of the music made me leap to my feet.		bald
5	His head is **without hair.**		wafer
6	The dress was made of **thin cloth.**		vowed
7	I ate a **thin biscuit** for lunch.		rhythm
8	The answer was **not clear.**		obscure
9	The **young bird** was eaten by the snake.		ruby
10	The steel rod is quite **easily bent.**		flexible
11	The newborn kittens are **without sight.**		muslin
12	She **promised** to be there by noon.		blind
13	The boys believed they had seen a **ghost.**		jasmine
14	She ruled a line down the **edge** of the page.		spectre
15	He was in a **jovial** mood.		brave
16	She began to **deride** the unfortunate person.		fledgling
17	We **dispersed** the seed in the soil.		jolly
18	As there is no wind the yachts are **motionless.**		scattered
19	She is a **valiant** soldier.		hate
20	I really **detest** this kind of food.		mock

TOTAL

/20

29

WRITTEN QUIZZES

PROVERBS

ENGLISH

One word in the right-hand list will complete each proverb correctly.
Can you find each and add them?

1	Birds of a _____ flock together.	loaf
2	A _____ in the hand is worth two in the bush.	wheel
3	Half a _____ is better than no bread.	smoke
4	Don't put all your _____ in one basket.	cloud
5	A small _____ will sink a great ship.	cooks
6	Where there's _____ there's fire.	apple
7	Let sleeping _____ lie.	late
8	Every _____ has a silver lining.	feather
9	Too many _____ spoil the broth.	eggs
10	New _____ sweep clean.	news
11	An_____ a day keeps the doctor away.	bird
12	God helps those who help _____.	vessels
13	Better _____ than never.	leak
14	No _____ is good news.	dogs
15	Set a _____ to catch a thief.	brooms
16	Still _____ runs deep.	sight
17	Out of _____ out of mind.	themselves
18	Empty _____ make the most noise.	thief
19	The squeaky _____ gets the grease.	work
20	All _____ and no play make Jack a dull boy.	water

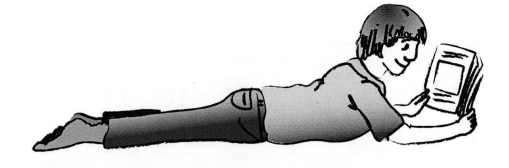

TOTAL

/20

30

WRITTEN QUIZZES

DATE _____

NAME _____

_____

HOMOPHONES

ENGLISH

You must write a homophone for the word in the boxes to fit in the spaces below.

1	pore	6	write	11	draft	16	rowed
2	waist	7	currant	12	medal	17	sore
3	higher	8	bow	13	principle	18	bored
4	wait	9	sight	14	stationary	19	check
5	find	10	groan	15	rains	20	pause

1   I tried to _____ the water into the glass.

2   We should never _____ good food.

3   Sam is going to _____ a machine to dig the holes.

4   A heavy _____ was needed to keep it secure.

5   The judge _____ the man fifty dollars.

6   Mike got all his sums _____.

7   A swift _____ carried the swimmers away.

8   The _____ of the tree broke and fell on the ground.

9   This is the _____ of the new tower.

10   The puppy has _____ a lot since I last saw him.

11   There was a strong _____ horse in the paddock.

12   You should not _____ in the affairs of others.

13   The _____ of our school came from Darwin.

14   We bought some _____ from the paper shop.

15   The jockey pulled hard on the _____ of the bridle.

16   Jack _____ the bike across the paddock.

17   We watched the jet _____ into the air.

18   I nailed a piece of _____ over the gap.

19   The man paid me with a _____ for one hundred dollars.

20   The dog favoured its injured _____.

TOTAL

/20

31

WRITTEN QUIZZES

SYNONYMS

ENGLISH

Choose a word from the box that is a synonym for a word below.
Colour each word as you use it.

strong	yearly	scarce	show
slim	sudden	rough	huge
horrible	waste	high	speed
height	ghost	part	short
round	weak	cheat	young

1	squander		11	youthful	
2	deceive		12	rare	
3	exhibit		13	gruesome	
4	robust		14	altitude	
5	annual		15	brief	
6	coarse		16	mammoth	
7	puny		17	lofty	
8	slender		18	abrupt	
9	portion		19	spectre	
10	velocity		20	circular	

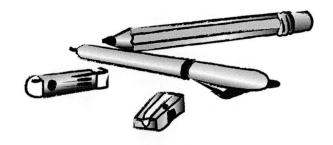

TOTAL

/20

32

WRITTEN QUIZZES

ANTONYMS

ENGLISH

Use a word from the right to fill the spaces with the correct opposite.

1	Some animals are thin while others may be _____.	opaque
2	She gave a good answer to my _____.	sour
3	Sugar is sweet but lemon is _____.	blunt
4	Mark is generous but Paul is _____.	common
5	This knife is sharp but this one is _____.	departure
6	This building is to be erected, while this one is to be _____.	genuine
7	This bird is rare but a sparrow is _____.	inferior
8	Our arrival time is ten o'clock. Our _____ time is noon.	hollow
9	This loaf of bread is stale but this one is _____.	stout
10	These jewels are artificial but these others are _____.	reject
11	Sam was found guilty but Tom was found _____.	demolished
12	He said he would accept the letter but _____ the parcel.	question
13	Lead is heavy but feathers are _____.	glut
14	These tree trunks are still solid but this one is_____.	innocent
15	Last year there was a famine but this year there is a _____ of wheat.	selfish
16	This building is ancient but this one is quite _____.	seldom
17	He often eats vegetables but _____ eat meat.	punished
18	Those children were rewarded for their behaviour but these children were _____.	fresh
19	This material is transparent while this one is _____.	light
20	These toys are superior to these _____ ones.	modern

TOTAL

/20

WRITTEN QUIZZES

TWIN WORDS

ENGLISH

Find a word in the grid that completes the word pairs below.

c	s	r	x	s	p	a	n	s	c	p	o	p	l
r	o	o	s	e	e	k	n	w	h	e	r	e	e
e	u	u	t	a	k	e	e	e	i	p	d	n	m
a	n	n	d	o	g	s	c	e	p	p	o	c	o
m	d	d	o	v	e	r	k	t	s	e	w	i	n
x	s	q	u	a	r	e	k	e	y	r	n	l	s
t	e	a	r	f	o	r	g	e	t	x	s	x	x

1	I ate fish and _____ for tea.	11	The horses raced neck and _____ down the straight.
2	I'm glad the speech was short and _____.	12	I put salt and _____ on my food.
3	Peter keeps his room spick and _____.	13	I've told you over and _____ not to do it.
4	The lost child was found safe and _____.	14	I put some jam and _____ on my scone.
5	They ran round and _____ the bushes.	15	The old car has had a lot of wear and _____.
6	He beat me fair and _____.	16	I'm prepared to forgive and _____.
7	We keep the jewels under lock and _____.	17	The party has been off and _____ all week.
8	The children played hide and _____.	18	I've had a lot of ups and _____ this week.
9	There has to be a little give and _____.	19	Mike said he has a pen and _____ in his desk.
10	It's raining cats and _____ at the moment.	20	We picked some oranges and _____.

34

WRITTEN QUIZZES

ANAGRAMS

ENGLISH

All the answers for the quiz can be found in the grid.
Find and colour the words in the grid and write these in the spots.

s	s	b	d	e	r	a	m	b	l	e	w	s
p	p	r	a	n	r	t	a	b	l	e	o	t
i	r	u	n	l	i	t	e	a	m	x	l	r
d	i	i	g	a	s	f	l	i	e	r	f	e
e	t	s	e	r	e	s	i	l	e	n	t	e
r	e	e	r	g	n	l	u	s	t	r	e	t
b	o	w	l	e	t	a	b	l	e	t	x	x
f	l	u	s	t	e	r	s	o	f	t	e	r
s	e	a	s	i	d	e	l	a	m	e	n	t

1	An anagram for flow is _____.	11	An anagram of siren is _____.
2	An anagram for marble is _____.	12	An anagram of rifle is _____.
3	An anagram for bleat is _____.	13	An anagram of tinsel is _____.
4	An anagram for mate can be meat, tame or _____.	14	An anagram of result is _____.
5	An anagram for prides is _____.	15	An anagram of battle is _____.
6	An anagram for priest is _____.	16	An anagram of restful is _____.
7	An anagram for rubies is _____.	17	An anagram of disease is _____.
8	An anagram of garden is _____.	18	An anagram of forest is _____.
9	An anagram of general is _____.	19	An anagram of setter is _____.
10	An anagram for blow is _____.	20	An anagram of mantle is_____.

TOTAL

/20

35

WRITTEN QUIZZES

DATE _____

NAME _____

_____

ANALOGIES

ENGLISH

All the answers for the quiz can be found in the grid.
Find a word in the grid to complete each analogy.

g	s	f	t	p	n	i	e	c	e	f	b	i
l	h	i	o	i	l	w	s	p	g	l	l	m
o	e	s	e	l	a	a	k	a	a	o	u	p
v	l	h	s	o	m	s	i	c	s	o	b	o
e	l	x	x	t	b	p	n	k	x	d	b	r
s	t	r	u	m	p	e	t	s	e	a	e	t
x	a	s	c	e	n	d	h	o	o	f	r	x
f	r	u	i	t	p	a	t	i	e	n	t	x

1	Wind is to hurricane as water is to_____.	11	Shoes are to feet as _____ are to hands.
2	Uncle is to nephew as Aunt is to_____.	12	Cat is to kitten as sheep is to _____.
3	Water is to steam as liquid is to _____.	13	Animal is to lion as insect is to _____.
4	Sheep is to flock as wolves are to _____.	14	Sheep is to mutton as whale is to _____.
5	Orange is to peel as banana is to _____.	15	Hand is to finger as foot is to _____.
6	Horse is to neigh as elephant is to _____.	16	Aeroplane is to air is ship is to _____.
7	Sailor is to ship as _____ is to plane.	17	Skink is to lizard as lemon is to _____.
8	Up is to down as _____ is to descend.	18	Teacher is to student as doctor is to _____.
9	Dog is to kennel as snail is to _____.	19	Paw is to dog as _____ is to horse.
10	Feathers are to bird as scales are to _____.	20	Out is to in as export is to _____.

TOTAL

/20

36

WRITTEN QUIZZES

DATE _____
NAME _____

AMERICAN WORDS

ENGLISH

Although Americans speak English many of the words they use for certain things differ from the words we use. Find the word in the grid and write it beside its Australian or New Zealand equivalent below.

f	h	o	b	o	c	a	n	d	y	e	c
a	s	o	d	a	a	u	t	o	j	l	o
u	f	o	o	t	b	a	l	l	e	e	o
c	d	r	u	g	g	i	s	t	r	v	k
e	v	a	c	a	t	i	o	n	k	a	i
t	s	t	r	e	e	t	c	a	r	t	e
s	i	d	e	w	a	l	k	x	p	o	s
s	c	h	e	d	u	l	e	t	u	r	r
a	p	a	r	t	m	e	n	t	m	j	o
t	r	a	s	h	m	u	t	t	p	e	c
b	a	g	g	a	g	e	x	r	s	y	k

1	soft drink _____		11	footpath _____
2	lollies _____		12	lift _____
3	gridiron _____		13	tramp _____
4	holiday _____		14	chemist _____
5	tap _____		15	flat _____
6	tram _____		16	rubbish _____
7	car _____		17	luggage _____
8	timetable _____		18	biscuits _____
9	jewel _____		19	stupid person _____
10	mongrel dog _____		20	dancing shoes _____

TOTAL

/20

37

WRITTEN QUIZZES

LANGUAGE 1

ENGLISH

Find the correct answers to the questions from the list on the right.

1	What name do we give to people who come from Wales?_____	water
2	What small boat is an anagram of ocean?_____	fungi
3	What collective noun do we use for a group of geese?_____	blue
4	For what does the abbreviation Hwy stand?_____	after
5	Complete this definition. A barge is a flat bottomed: _____	canoe
6	What kind of creature is a cassowary?_____	boat
7	What word beginning with l means the opposite of enslave?_____	bird
8	Insomnia is the inability to: _____	Welsh
9	Complete this analogy: osprey is to bird as lynx is to: _____	cat
10	What word beginning with s means the same as astonished?_____	gaggle
11	Complete this proverb. A stitch in time saves: _____	sleep
12	What adjective can be made from the word terror? _____	mustard
13	What small word can we add to straw to make a compound word?_____	surprised
14	Add a word to complete this simile. As keen as: _____	liberate
15	Which of these words would come first in a dictionary? massage, mason, mascot, mastodon, masquerade_____	nine
16	What is the plural of fungus?_____	highway
17	What noun can be made from the word beautiful?_____	beauty
18	Complete this definition: ultramarine is a deep _____colour.	berry
19	What does the prefix 'post' mean? E.g. postmortem _____	terrible
20	The latin root word aqua has what meaning?_____	mascot

TOTAL

/20

38

WRITTEN QUIZZES

DATE _____

NAME _____

_____

LANGUAGE 2

ENGLISH

Find the correct answers to the questions from the list on the right.

1	The suffix 'ette', found in words such as cigarette and laundrette, means what?_____	Tanzania
2	The prefix prime or primus has what meaning?_____.	little
3	Complete this proverb. When the cat's away, the _____ will play.	well
4	What portmanteau word has been made from the words smoke and fog?_____.	first
5	What country do people known as Tanzanians come from?_____	transparent
6	What kind of creature is a puffin?_____	phenomenon
7	Beginning with t, what is the opposite of opaque?_____	mice
8	What is the singular form of phenomena? _____	bird
9	Complete this definition. A tarantula is a large, poisonous_____	spider
10	Beginning with a, what word means the same as home or dwelling?_____	abode
11	The abbreviation NB stand for nota bene which means note:_____	smog
12	What name is given to a room in which surgeons perform operations?_____	bow
13	What term do Americans use for a tap?_____	theatre
14	What word can we add to rain to made a compound word?_____	faucet
15	For what word is fridge an abbreviation?_____	army
16	What collective noun do we use for a large group of frogs?_____	refrigerator
17	What name do we give to the fear of enclosed spaces?_____	circuses
18	From what verb does the noun description come?_____	customary
19	What adjective can be made from the noun custom?_____	describe
20	What is the plural of circus?_____	claustrophobia

TOTAL

/20

39

WRITTEN QUIZZES

MATHS MIX 1

MATHS

Find the correct answers to the questions from the list on the right.

1	How many days are there in three fortnights?_____	24
2	What is ¾ written as a percentage?_____	13
3	20% of ten dollars is what amount?_____	23
4	What number multiplied by 9 makes 207?_____	42
5	What name do we give to half a semi-circle?_____	200
6	How many years in 4 ½ decades?_____	quadrant
7	What numbers comes exactly half way between 61 and 71? _____	66
8	What is the answer when you divide XXX by VI?:_____	V (5)
9	What is 15 more than the number that is 5 more than 16?_____	670
10	How many years does a bicentenary represent?_____	45
11	What is the answer when you subtract half of 260 from twice 400?_____	36
12	If 1 centimetre represents 100 metres on a map, what length would represent 450 metres?_____	$2
13	How many minutes are there between 4.08 pm and 6.12 pm?_____	4.5 cm
14	Double 2538._____	75%
15	What number comes next in this pattern: 60, 120, 180, 240,…_____	124
16	The area of a square is 100cm². What are the length of its sides?_____	300
17	How many prime numbers are there between 10 and 20? _____	5076
18	How many sides have 8 hexagons?_____	10cm
19	A cricketer has scored 87 runs. How many more to make a century?_____	4
20	What is our numeral for XXIV?_____	48

TOTAL

/20

40

DATE	_____
NAME	_____

MATHS MIX 2

MATHS

Find the correct answers to the questions from the list on the right.

1	What is the sum of 36 and 38? _____	91
2	What is the difference between 208 and 39?_____.	169
3	What are the total number of days in April, May and June?_____	36
4	A square is 9cm long. How many centimeters is its perimeter?_____.	74
5	How many hours from 8am to 3pm?_____	700
6	It is 3.55pm. What was the time 6 minutes ago?_____	7
7	What is the largest number (in our numbers) that you can make by arranging the Roman numerals X, X, C, and V? _____	3.49pm
8	What is the answer when you subtract 400 from twice 550? _____	125
9	How many sides have eight octagons?_____	85
10	How many prime numbers between 30 and 40?_____	18
11	What number between 10 and 20 when doubled and then added to 14 equals 50?_____	64
12	How many years in 8 ½ decades?_____	2
13	What is the value of 6 in 276,421?_____	80
14	At least how old is an octogenarian?_____	2000
15	Round off 1540 to the nearest 1000. _____	6000
16	What is double 535?	1070
17	What is the difference between half of 70 and half of 150?	40
18	What fraction of a kilometre is 500 metres?_____	½
19	What number comes next in this pattern 7, 14, 22, 31, 41,…?_____	52
20	After 2008, what will be the next leap year? _____	2012

TOTAL

/20

41

DATE _____

NAME _____

_____

IT ALL ADDS UP

MATHEMATICS

Find the correct answer to each question from the list on the right.

1	The sum of 45 and 46 is _____.	278
2	The number that is 60 more than 84 is _____.	216
3	The number that is 27 more than 5^2 is _____.	25
4	What is the total number of legs on 8 spiders and 8 beetles? _____.	125
5	The sum of all the odd numbers between 80 and 90 is _____.	112
6	Add 35 to 8^2 and you get _____.	135
7	The number 105 more than 1/3 of 90 is _____.	91
8	The total when you add all the even numbers between 11 and 21 is _____.	174
9	What is two dozen more than 150? _____.	127
10	What is the answer in Arabic numbers when you add XXXV and IX? _____.	52
11	What is ten more than the sum of 643 and 258? _____.	91
12	Tom is 18, Mike 17, and Sally 19. The total of their age is _____.	17
13	The total when you add 5.3, 6.2 and 5.5 is _____.	144
14	What is half of the sum of 66, 82 and 90? _____.	80
15	What is the answer if you add 46 and 93 then double it? _____.	54
16	Peter's grandfather is 73 years older than Peter who is 18 years old. His grandfather is _____ years of age.	425
17	The total of 32, 63 and 19 plus a bakers dozen is _____.	44
18	If x=45, y=26 and z=54 what does x+y+z equal? _____.	99
19	The sum of 3^2 and 4^2 is _____.	119
20	To the sum of 48 and 68, add the number 10 more than 90. _____.	911

TOTAL

/20

42

WRITTEN QUIZZES

DATE _____

NAME

_____

SUBTRACTION

MATHEMATICS

Find the correct answer to each question from the list on the right.

1	Seven dozen minus 8 is _____.	40
2	The number 85 less than 600 is _____.	180
3	Sixty minus half of 40 is _____.	9
4	$6^2 - 3^2 =$ _____.	76
5	Subtract the number 3 less than 48 from 60 and your answer is _____.	42
6	What is 400 minus half of 236? _____.	515
7	How many years are there from 1942 to 1998? _____.	173
8	What is the result when you take the number of minutes in 2 hours from the number of minutes in 5 hours? _____.	27
9	The difference between 88.4 and 26.5 is _____.	19
10	92 minus 40 is _____.	15
11	If x=100, y=26 and z=15 then x-y-z= _____.	56
12	I have 27 swap cards. I need _____ more to make 200.	282
13	I had 127 swap cards and gave away 93. I have _____ left.	47
14	Find the missing number: 49–10= 60 -_____?	61.9
15	The number 6 less than 5^2 is _____?	293
16	A car is travelling to a city 350kms away. It has already covered 57kms. It still has _____ kilometres to go.	52
17	The difference between six dozen and the number of days in June is _____.	34
18	The answer to XXXIV – XXV is _____.	59
19	What is the difference between 5 dozen and one bakers dozen? _____.	17
20	The difference between the total number of days in June, July and August and the number of minutes in 1 ¼ hours is? _____.	21

TOTAL

/20

43

WRITTEN QUIZZES

MATHS TERMS

MATHEMATICS

Add a word from the box below in the correct space.

1   The particular characteristics of an object, such as its size, shape, colour, etc. is known as its _____.

2   The opposite direction to which the hands of a clock move is _____.

3   Symbols that group things, such as numbers, together are called _____

4   If two numbers have the same value they are said to be _____.

5   A rough calculation is an _____.

6   A line in which no part is straight is called a _____.

7   A unit used for measuring things such as temperature or the size of an angle is called a _____.

8   The branch of mathematics dealing with space and shape is called _____.

9   A part of a whole number is called a _____.

10   A statement about numbers using numerals and symbols is called a number _____.

11   A number that when divided by 2 leaves a remainder is called an _____ number.

12   To take away or find the difference between numbers is to _____.

13   When a number is divided by another unevenly the amount left over is called the _____.

14   The position of a digit in a number indicating its value is called its _____ value.

15   The distance around the outside of a shape is called its _____.

16   A shape is said to have _____ when one half will fit exactly over the other.

17   Any of the set of non-fractional numbers greater than zero e.g. 1,2,3,4,5, are called _____numbers.

18   The distance from the centre of a circle to its circumference is called its _____.

19   The answer to a division problem is called the _____.

20   A graph that uses pictures to represent information is called a _____.

estimate	brackets	curve	geometry	place
sentence	odd	pictograph	symmetry	equivalent
subtract	fraction	attributes	degree	remainder
quotient	radius	perimeter	whole	anticlockwise

TOTAL

/20

44

WRITTEN QUIZZES

DATE _____

NAME _____

_____

MONEY

MATHEMATICS

Add a word from the box below in the correct space.

1   The currency of what country is nicknamed the "green back"?_____.

2   The European Union now largely uses which unit of currency?_____.

3   The different amounts of notes and coins are known as what?_____.

4   The major currency of which country was historically the franc? _____.

5   The drachma was an ancient (and modern) currency of what country?_____.

6   There are one _____ cents in ten dollars.

7   The important metal in our monetary system is _____.

8   If pencils cost 90c each, two boxes of 20 will cost _____.

9   I have $5.50. I need _____ to have $20.00.

10   If I spend half of $46.50 how much do I have left?_____.

11   The cost of 1 ½ dozen apples at 10 cents each is _____.

12   Trading goods and services without exchanging money is called what?_____.

13   The cost of 3 frozen chickens at $5.60 each is _____.

14   A container for notes is called a _____.

15   What is 50% of $18.60? _____.

16   Our system of money is called the _____ system.

17   Our major monetary unit is the dollar but in England it is the _____.

18   The major unit of money in Russia is the _____

19   Joel has $8.50 but Mike has $14.50 more than Joel.
     How much money has Mike got? _____.

20   Instead of using cash or credit cards we can use
     a money order called a _____.

The U.S.A	$36.00	$16.80	$9.30	gold
thousand	France	barter	$1.80	Euro
$23.25	Greece	denominations	$14.50	decimal
$23.00	wallet	pound	rouble	cheque

TOTAL

/20

WRITTEN QUIZZES

DATE _____

NAME _____
_____

CHALLENGE MATHS

MATHEMATICS

Colour the box that contains the correct answer.

1	What is the sum of 78 and 62?	138	140	145
2	What number is eight more than 67?	74	80	75
3	What number is 5^2 minus 3?	22	23	24
4	How many years are there from 1896 to 1958?	48	50	62
5	How many years in two centuries and 5 decades?	200	250	300
6	What is 150 more than 1/3 of 90?	180	280	140
7	What is ¼ of 60?	18	20	15
8	What number is 40 more than half of 206?	113	140	143
9	What is the difference between 10^2 and 5^2?	75	70	105
10	How many legs altogether have 8 spiders and 3 beetles?	80	82	79
11	How many sides altogether have 5 octagons and 6 pentagons?	170	68	70
12	What is 20 less than double 45?	70	100	65
13	What is the result when you subtract 89 from 101?	12	13	11
14	What number is 60 more than half of 32?	76	70	74
15	How many quarters in 5 ¾?	20	21	23
16	Add half of 18 to half of 46.	32	33	42
17	How many minutes are there in 2 ¼ hours?	135	160	145
18	What is the product of 4 and 48?	202	192	190
19	What number is 8 less than half of 66?	25	35	45
20	How many 6 cent lollies can you buy for $3.36?	55	56	66

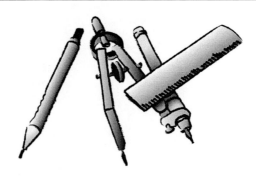

TOTAL

/20

46

WRITTEN QUIZZES

DATE	_____
NAME	
_____	

MATHS WORD FINDER

MATHEMATICS

A	B	C	D	E	F	G	H	I	J	K	L	M
90	18	84	200	56	400	11	70	33	101	60	140	111
N	O	P	Q	R	S	T	U	V	W	X	Y	Z
85	100	91	31	120	40	71	14	13	119	17	131	61

Work out each table fact then add the four in each column together. Now use the code to find the corresponding letter to discover the names of the common things.

1

4 x 10	40 / 2	5 x 5	7 x 3	4 x 3
24 / 4	6 x 4	4 x 8	30 / 2	16 / 8
4 x 4	100 / 10	16 + 8	5 x 4	8 x 3
12 + 17	4 x 4	11 + 8	10 + 19	9 x 2

2

90 / 10	7 x 7	3 x 3	42 / 6	5 x 5
8 x 5	8 x 6	20 / 10	8 x 8	4 x 3
6 x 3	4 x 5	13 - 11	2 x 2	20 / 4
28 / 7	10 - 7	100 / 100	3^2	6 x 3

3

8 x 6	24 + 29	40 x 3	36/4	7 x 4
7 x 9	5 x 4	6 x 6	20 / 4	3 x 12
12 / 4	72 / 8	63 / 7	64 / 8	42 / 6
36 / 6	64 / 8	5 x 7	6 + 5	54-25

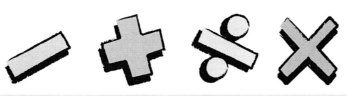

TOTAL

/20

47

WRITTEN QUIZZES

MYSTERY CREATURE

MATHEMATICS

Complete the calculations then use the letters code to discover the creature reading downwards.

A	B	C	D	E	F	G	H	I	J	K	L	M
27	15	9	200	70	49	36	20	11	19	31	51	14
N	O	P	Q	R	S	T	U	V	W	X	Y	Z
90	33	8	17	40	100	48	55	12	150	45	35	1000

1	$4 \times 15 - 3 \times 4 =$	
2	$5^2 + 10 =$	
3	XVI + XXIV =	
4	$6^2 - 9 =$	
5	$8 \times 8 + 2 \times 13 =$	
6	Double 18 then add half of 108 =	
7	Double 8 then add half of 34 =	
8	To 5 dozen add half of 80 =	
9	Years in 2 decades plus half of 14 =	
10	100 subtract half of 90 =	
11	Subtract 20 from half of 120 =	
12	Double 20 and add half of 30 =	
13	5/10 of 90 then add 11 times 5 =	
14	Two dozen then add half of 32 =	
15	Double 90 and subtract the half of 220 =	
16	Halve the difference between 100 and 10 =	

TOTAL

/ 20

48